AF255888

Books may be purchased in quantity and/or special sales by contacting the publisher, Cardboard Clouds LLC, at www.cardboardclouds.com or by email at hello@cardboardclouds.com.

Published by: Cardboard Clouds LLC
Written by: Dontavious Pittman
Illustrated by: Max Rambaldi
ISBN 13: 978-0-692-94215-4
First Edition

I didn't ask to be CREATIVE

Written by
Dontavious Pittman

Illustrated by
Max Rambaldi

Published by
Cardboard Clouds LLC

Kyle, you're the captain of this ship. Are you ready for the task? I know you are only eight, but you'll do great. Need help? I'm here, just ask.

Hi guys. What's with all of the mess? It looks like you're having a blast.
Is this the box that was out at the road? The one I placed by the trash?

Yes, this morning Kyle found the box and I helped him get it clean.
After bending, cutting, and gluing it, we have a submarine.

A submarine? Is that what it is? I never would have guessed. I'm about to go make dinner. Be sure to tidy up the mess.

Remember when you were a girl? You did such creative things. You painted pretty pictures, and you really liked to sing. I remember that an artist or celebrity is what you wanted to become.

Dad, that was so long ago, my creativity is done. Yes, I used to dream of making things for the entire world to see, and even being someone's favorite actress on tv. But I lost the will to chase a dream that wasn't meant for me.

I wish that I could be creative, but I never have the time. Even with work and taking care of Kyle, it's always on my mind.

If only I could find the time to try out something new... But who am I kiddin'? At my age there is nothing left for me to do.

Is it me that is keeping her from trying something new? She works so hard to be a mom, and now she's feeling blue.

All mom does is grown-up stuff, and never wants to play. If it doesn't change, the fun inside of her will go away.

I don't like it when she's sad, It always gets me down. I have to show her the world of creativity around.

If I show her how I see things, it should get the juices flowing. Then the imagination will reappear without her even knowing.

Rise and shine my fun Loving kid. It's time to start the day. Grandpa is on his way back home, It stinks that he couldn't stay.

I know you guys had fun together, playing a lot of games. I just wish that I were a little creative, so we could do the same. How do you do it?

Well...I didn't ask to be creative,
it's what I was born to be.
I'd rather step outside of the box,
then do things normally.

I wake up to a different beat
with music everywhere.
I make guitars out of air,
while my stage is just a chair.

Little boy, with your imagination,
get down and make your bed.
Be careful with the jumping son,
before you break your leg.

Today we have a list of chores,
I'd like to get them done.
After all of the work is finished,
we can have a little fun.

Why make my bed? When I can be a pirate and sail the floor beneath. Searching for the sunken treasure before I brush me teeth. I need someone to man the deck. Would you care to be my mate?

Not this second, we have things to do. The fun will have to wait.

I'm about to go make breakfast. Get dressed so you can eat. Once again, please make up your bed and be sure to brush your teeth!

While you serve my breakfast,
I'll imagine I'm a king.
Waiting for a lovely feast,
my servant has to bring.

Servant? Very funny son. In this house I'm the queen. Eat up so we can shake a leg, and get in the swing of things.

It feels like we are stuck in space...

Just orbiting around.

This traffic is like a black hole..

Where a horn is the only SOUND!

Black hole?
Orbit?
All I see are cars.
The sky is still a blue sky...
And we haven't gone that far.

Look! That cloud looks like an elephant And that one is a pear. Can we stay outside a little longer? There are cool shapes everywhere!

Sorry son, we are on a mission. We
need to hurry fast. Besides those
clouds just look like cotton and
balls of blurry gas.

MARKET

Some things in this world can't just be looked at with your eyes.

If you squint and open up your heart, You may be surprised.
When you get to be my age, the world can make you blind. You pay a price for creativity and sometimes you lose your mind.

Listen, I wish I
were creative, but
I just wasn't
meant to be.
Painting pictures,
arts and crafts,
that stuff wasn't
meant for me.

It's not all about making art, It's about the way you live. How you can make the world a better place, and what you have to give... But it seems like you're done giving.

Hmm....
I have some extra time, now that the food is placed away. After I tidy up this mess I'm going to call the rest a day.

But wait...
I can use this stuff, I can't
just throw it all away...
Maybe Kyle was on to
something earlier today.
KYLE!!! GUESS WHAT!

You're my gift to this world son.
Now here's my gift to you,
for showing me creativity and
believing in me too.
Even if I don't become an artist,
or find something else to do...

MY Dreams
will always be ALIVE
because of all of ME
in YOU!